Move Over!

Teenage Manners Coming Through

Steff Steinhorst

Illustrated by Jake Knapp

For Alyssa

from Steff

Resource Publications, Inc.
San Jose, California

Reprint Department
Resource Publications, Inc.
160 E. Virginia Street #290
San Jose, CA 95112-5876
(408) 286-8505 voice
(408) 287-8748 fax

Library of Congress Cataloging-in-Publication Data
Steinhorst, Steff, 1938–
    Move over! : teenage manners coming through / Steff Steinhorst.
        p.   cm.
    Includes bibliographical references.
    Summary: Discusses why manners are important and offers advice on proper behavior in a variety of situations.
    ISBN 0-89390-535-6
    1. Etiquette for children and teenagers. [1. Etiquette.] I. Title.

BJ1857.C5 .S74 2001
395.1'23—dc21

                                                                2001031930

01 02 03 04 05 | 5 4 3 2 1

Editorial director: Nick Wagner
Editor: Ken Guentert
Production: Romina Saha
Copyeditor: Tricia Joerger
Cover design: Mike Sagara, Nelson Estarija

Dedicated
to
My sweet Mother-in-law,
Harriet Clayton,
Who believes in manners

Contents

Acknowledgments

I'd like to begin by thanking the world's best editor, Ken Guentert, for envisioning this project. This book was his idea.

Next, thanks to all those kids in my classes who were in on the book from the start and who had all kinds of helpful suggestions. I told them their names would be in the book and they are: Amy Berdan, Isla Beckner, Christa Harvey, Michelle Troutman, Alice Evans, Pam Conners, Jennifer Scheckel, Hillary Rancourt, Becky LaPorte, Amber Langworthy, Amber Johannek, Rose Sharp, Shannon Grace, Jeff Harris, Mike Walker, Wiley Simoneon, Isaac Frausto, Michael O'Grady, Rory Sholl, James Mohler, Jason Green, Dustin Fox, Eric Woodruff, Sadie Hawkins, Moses Zderic and Mallory Dimich.

My younger but wiser sister-in-law, Janice Clayton, is always a help in whatever I do and deserves thanks. The Hansen sisters, Harriet and Charlotte, are as mannerly as they come and can be counted on to shed light on the subject. Thanks to Antje Wortman for her insights on manners and life in general. And thanks to my best buddy, Mike Parnell, who lets me act any way I want.

Acknowledgment also to my nephew, Christopher Lucia.

And, finally, thanks to my wife, Charlotte, who is the most supportive person one could ever hope for and who always treats me right.

Introduction

A recent survey of high school students revealed that, on a scale of one to ten, teenage manners ranked somewhere between two and five. You know their manners are not what they could be or should be.

According to teens, the reasons for such a low self-rating are three-fold:

- Parents do not teach or model good manners.
- Manners are not as important as they used to be.
- Teenagers just don't care.

The purpose of this book, written for teens with their advice, is to talk about manners, explain why manners are important, and provide you with help when and where you need it most.

Chapter 1

Do Not Pick
The Nose

What manners used to be

She wasn't "cute." She wasn't "pretty." She was absolutely the most beautiful girl in the sixth grade, if not in the whole world, and I couldn't take my eyes off her. She had shoulder-length brown hair, sparkling eyes, and a smile so dazzling it blinded. My seat was a few rows back from hers and to the side. I used to position myself to look at her with what felt like a drooling, slack-jawed grin. Trance-like. Then one October afternoon I stared as she slipped her index finger up her right nostril. It wasn't a subtle nose pick; it was a trophy hunt. And a successful one at that. I watched her withdraw a sticky, wet booger nearly half an inch long. She held it in front of her contemplating it as if it were an inch worm balanced on the tip of one's finger. And then she ate it.

I was horrified. My attraction to her vanished like the air in an exploded balloon. Questions ran through my mind. Did she do this all the time? Did she not think someone might bear witness to this vulgarity or did she just not care? Had she no manners?

In 1917 a book was published for schools to train students in common courtesies. One of the rules was: Do Not Pick the Nose. My friend did not know this rule. But the manners of the past can be laughable in today's world. Old-fashioned admonitions just wouldn't cut it in the twenty first century. For example, what would you say if you were told to keep a clean handkerchief? Who even keeps a handkerchief any more? The thought of stuffing a snot-filled hanky into one's pocket grosses out most people. Facial tissues have been invented, never mind that everybody expects someone else to provide them. In case you're thinking that expectations for teenagers today are far too high, enjoy some of these "rules" from early in the last century. *Remember*: These are from 1917—except for the boldface headings. Those are my comments.

What kind of friend can't put up with my BO?

Since we must look at one another as we work and play together, we ought to look as clean as possible; the cleaner we are the better we look.

Who carries a fingernail clipper today?

Every self-respecting boy and girl should clean the nails at least once a day.

More than you wanted to know about nose care

Not only the outside of the nose should be bathed but also the inside, for the nostrils catch much dust. If the nose is not kept clean an itching may be felt, and this itching causes some children to pick the nose. This is not cleanly. Never pick the nose. Strange to say, there are people who do not use their handkerchiefs. Such people are very unpleasant companions. A piece of plain, white cloth, neatly hemmed, looks better and shows more refinement than a soiled handkerchief, even if the soiled one is made of fine linen or silk and trimmed with lace.

But what about spiked and purple hair?

Because boys wear the hair short it is easier for them than for girls to keep it clean; boys can wash the head oftener than girls. About once in two weeks is sufficiently often for girls to wash their hair. Would it not be fine if every boy and every girl in the United States took pride in having a clean scalp and clean hair?

No, you can't borrow my toothbrush.

Sometimes we turn our heads away when certain people come too near us, because we dislike the odor of their breath. I wonder if you have a bad breath. Save your pennies and buy a good toothbrush. Everybody should own his own toothbrush. Never use another person's toothbrush.

And there is nothing about "chew" that is mannerly.

People who are truly cleanly never, under any circumstances, spit upon the floor or upon the steps of a building, in the street cars, or on the sidewalk. If they find it necessary to spit they use the handkerchief.

And not a thing about braces

It is bad manners to hold things in the mouth, like pennies or nickels, to chew the ends of pencils, to suck or lick the fingers, or to put ink on the lips or tongue. What kind of a "picture" do you make when you soil your mouth by chewing pencils, or sucking or licking your fingers? To some people you are very repulsive when you get your mouth dirty; they do not like to look at you.

You lose sleep over these, don't you?

If you are a boy, tie your necktie carefully. If you are a girl, make your ribbon bows look neat and jaunty.

See anything here that is "politically incorrect"?

Be kind to the unfortunate. Do not tease a foolish, half-witted boy or girl, nor laugh at a deformed schoolfellow. If you are sound in mind and body, be thankful and show your thankfulness by treating the afflicted kindly. If one of the pupils in your school is a hunchback or a cripple, be careful not to mention his deformity. Try to have him enter into your sports as much as possible and make him forget that he is a cripple.

No fair making fun of these. Some would really help.

What to Do:

1. Come to school on time, wearing as clean clothing as possible, with face and hands and neck and ears washed, teeth brushed, nails cleaned, shoes polished, and hair neatly brushed and combed. If you come bare-footed, see that your feet are as clean as possible.
2. Be cheerful. Say "Good morning" and "Good night" to your teacher and to your schoolmates.
3. Treat the school buildings and the school furniture with respect. Talk and move quietly in the schoolhouse whether school is in session or not. If you are a boy, take off your hat when you enter the door of the school building.
4. Treat the school grounds with respect. Throw all pieces of paper, scraps of food, etc., into the garbage can.

5. Be kind to the younger and weaker boys and girls, to those who are crippled, to strangers and foreigners and to all others who need your help.

6. If you are a boy, be respectful to ladies and to girls. Raise your hat when you greet them. Stand aside to let them pass out of a doorway first. Carry heavy bundles for them.

7. If you are a girl, receive the attention of boys courteously. Always say "Thank you" distinctly, so they can hear you, whenever boys have done favors for you, such as opening doors, carrying parcels, or handing you something you have dropped.

8. Stand and walk with head erect and shoulders thrown back.

9. Lift your feet in walking; have a spring in your step.

10. Look people straight in the eyes.

11. Repeat to your friends the pleasant things you hear said of them and try to forget the unpleasant ones.

12. Be thoughtful of schoolmates who are ill and out of school. Write to them. If possible send them flowers or other little gifts. Perhaps, unless ill with a contagious disease, you can visit them.

We'd like to think you know better.

What Not to Do:

1. Do not pout when asked to do something which seems unpleasant.

2. Do not tease those who are deformed or crippled or any who are weaker than yourself.

3. Do not laugh at the mistakes or failures of others.
4. Do not boast when you win in a contest.
5. Do not crowd or push through doorways.
6. Do not look over another's shoulder to see what he is reading or writing.
7. Do not interrupt a person speaking.
8. Do not flatly contradict anyone.
9. Do not listen at doors or windows to conversations which you are not expected to overhear.
10. Do not rudely stare at strangers nor question them curiously about their private affairs.
11. Do not talk nor laugh noisily nor play roughly in the school building.
12. Do not spit on the floor or on any part of the school building or buildings.
13. Do not forget to have a clean handkerchief nor to use it when necessary.

Questions to think about

- Were these the good old days?
- Which ones are still appropriate today?
- Would it be better or worse if we returned to these behaviors and why?

Chapter 2

Moody, Rude, And Tattooed

The state of teenage manners

The Ugly American was a popular book in the late fifties and early sixties. It talked about American behavior abroad and how its inconsideration of others appalled the rest of the world. In many ways teenagers leave the same impression on the general public.

It's not intentional.

Teenagers are hard to ignore. The clothes, the hair, the body piercings, the type and volume of the music, and the tattoos all call attention to a teenager. And that may be the point of it all.

But adults get negative impressions of teens when they:

- are noisy in public
- litter
- crowd into lines or don't give the right of way
- walk between a person and what they are looking at (for example, a book on a library shelf or a product on a supermarket shelf)
- walk between two people talking without asking to be excused
- drive impolitely (for example, tailgating or cutting in too closely)
- interrupt
- forget to say "please" or "excuse me"
- use bad language in public
- purposely annoy friends or siblings for the sport of it
- make out, lip lock, or otherwise demonstrate public passionate displays of unbridled emotions
- behave rudely to waiters, clerks, or other service people

The list can go on and on because teenagers are so creative in their transgressions—and adults are so limited in their ability to anticipate them.

There are a few areas of teenage life that are difficult for adults to ignore.

Your wardrobe

I enjoy asking teenagers if they would be willing to wear a school uniform. The answer always comes back as a resounding "No!" What amuses me is that uniforms are so much a part of my students' lives. Baggy pants low on the hips, a T-shirt with a brand name, and a baseball hat on either forwards or backwards—that was my students' chosen uniform when I wrote this. By the time you read this, the favored uniform will be something else. In my lifetime, I'm half-expecting to see every teen in my town wearing underwear as headgear. Everything else has been done. Clothes send a message. We are either hip or traditional, or we thumb our noses at tradition. We send signals that we have pride in our clothes because they are expensive, or we are proud that we are thrifty and get our clothes from the used clothes discount store. We want to be noticed, or we want to blend. We are either neat and clean, or we are slobs—but really, really comfortable (or are we?).

Some questions to consider:

- Does the way you feel affect the way you act?
- Does the way you dress affect the way you feel?
- Do people treat you differently depending on the way you're dressed?

Take your time and think about the answers. The way you dress may very well change your behavior—and the people you meet. Deep down you probably know that—you dress the way you do at least some of the time to get a reaction. From your parents. From the opposite sex. You already know the power of clothing. If you pay more attention to this power, your life may go more smoothly.

Some guidelines that might help:

- If you are with your peers, anything goes. Go ahead and wear the "uniform." The object is to be comfortable and feel that you belong.
- If you are hanging out at home, going to school, attending worship services, applying for a job, eating in anything but a fast food restaurant, respect the dress code set by your parents or other adults in charge. You're on their turf, not yours.
- A big issue is that baseball hat. Hats should simply not be worn indoors despite the fact that the practice is much more common than ever. This is especially true in restaurants and theaters. And be sure to remove it during the playing of the "Star Spangled Banner" or the reciting of the "Pledge of Allegiance." Look around next time you're at a game. Even many adults ignore this guideline. (But not if they've been in the military.)

Your music

Now take that boom box. Please. It may surprise you but not everyone thinks your music is terrific. You like the beat and you like those in-your-face lyrics. That's okay.

Parents may think your music is unhealthy. Remind them that adults of the time felt the same way about Frank Sinatra and the Beatles. This too shall pass.

The only crime is forcing your music on the ears of people who don't want to listen to it. You wouldn't appreciate being forced to listen to music you don't like. So play the music as loud as you want—as long as others can't hear it. (And yes, there are a few so-called adults who need to get this message as well.)

Your language

Speaking of volume, listen to yourselves talk. You're creative, using what approaches a language all its own. You're outrageous. You're fun. You're loud. If you're among friends, no big deal. If you're distracting others by being too loud—or too vulgar—you're being rude. Check your language. Be considerate of others *for your sake*.

Freedom?

Some teenagers—some adults for that matter—don't care what other people think. They will argue that acting any way you choose is the ultimate freedom. But if someone's actions infringe on your rights, then their behavior is wrong. And if you're doing what you want—and annoying someone else in the process—then you might just be wrong. And people may tell you so.

Manners are a way to go about your business without getting into trouble with everyone around you. Manners are a good deal—*for you.*

Chapter 3

What's In It For Me?

Why manners are important

Once you accept that it is in your best interest to demonstrate good manners, the idea of "minding your manners" becomes easier to swallow. Does money motivate you? Does catching that certain person's eye matter? Are you interested in not making a fool of yourself?

I have good news for you. Politeness works. For example, you could try making points with your parents, your boss, or your teacher by doing extra work. Or you could try being polite. The latter is easier—and you'll get just as many points.

Whatever it is you want out of life, good manners will help you get it—unless your goal in life is to get beaten up countless times, or to get free room and board in prison, or to lose that special someone you'd like to date, or to get fired from every job you've ever had. If you're interested in those things, good manners will just get in your way.

It's okay to be selfish about manners and ask, "What's in it for me?" If you understand that good manners are in your best interest, you will be more motivated to be on your best behavior. Ten reasons for having good manners:

1. Polite people are better looking than rude people.
2. Your chances of attracting that special someone will increase about a million percent.
3. People will want to hire you.
4. Or give you a raise.
5. Adults won't yell at you. As much.
6. Dogs won't bite you.
7. Referees won't call as many fouls on you.
8. Little kids won't kick you in the shins.

9. Her or his parents will want you to be part of the family.
10. You'll get more playing time.

Good reasons, don't you think? But we're not through. Ten more reasons for having good manners:

11. Teachers will give you better grades.
12. You'll have more friends.
13. You won't embarrass yourself in "formal" situations.
14. Or the people you are with.
15. You won't appear too stupid to know any better.
16. You'll feel better about yourself.
17. You'll make tense situations calmer.
18. You can avoid being shot for "dissing" someone.
19. Manners make others feel good.
20. Manners are free.

I like to look at both sides of every issue. Four reasons to ignore good behavior:

1. You can get fired from every job you'll ever have.
2. You can get beaten up. Constantly.
3. You can lose every one you've ever loved.
4. You can have a lifetime of security with free room and board. In prison.

Add it all up and it is a real no-brainer. It pays to behave.

Chapter 4

Manners Among Friends

Are you kidding?

Ever wonder why some kids have lots of friends and others have hardly any?

Friends are important to teenagers. Surveys show that peer approval is more important to most teenagers than teacher approval or even parental approval. This helps to explain why teenagers act the way they do. If making and keeping friends is a major goal in your life, you will behave in ways that help you have friends. Usually. Curiously, if you are like most other teens, you sometimes behave in ways that hurt your relationships with your friends. This is one area where a few manners can be a big help.

When I ask teens which manners are important among friends, they usually look at me like I've asked the dumbest question imaginable. Duh. After all, that's *why* you have friends—so you can be "yourself." You can act any way you want, and a friend will still be your friend.

But that doesn't mean you can treat your friends any way you want. There are some things that you can do and some things you can't—at least if you want to keep your friends. For a friendship to develop there has to be an equal exchange of who you are. How much of yourself, how many of your secrets, are you willing to share? This requires a level of trust not found in casual relationships. Too often we love things and use people when it should be the other way around.

Some things to do to make friends:

- Be pleasant so people want to meet you.
- People are attracted to positive, upbeat people. At parties and dances, have fun. Some people act "down" to get sympathy. Don't do that.

- Be careful about complaining about all the things going wrong in your life.
- Show genuine interest in the people you meet.

Once you have met someone you like, there are ways to solidify a relationship:

- Invite the person to a meal.
- Put as much or more into the relationship than you are getting from it.
- Rise in defense of good friends when they are criticized. Be loyal.
- Check in with friends on a regular basis.
- Be ready to help in an emergency, short or long term.
- Be sensitive to a friend's emotions.
- Never ask too much of each other.
- Compromise on what you do together.
- Remember and respect what is important to the other.
- Enjoy surprising each other with creative acts of kindness.

As reported by teenagers themselves, some basic manners to observe among friends include:

- Don't take stuff without asking. Don't reach across the table and grab and eat those last four French fries from your friend. Don't mess with a friend's food.
- Don't borrow clothes without asking. And if you do borrow clothes, return them *clean*.

- Don't be a backstabber. Talking behind someone's back usually gets back to the person you're talking about. It is not cool to spread gossip.
- Don't be phony and put on a front just to impress people. Be yourself.
- Don't "use" friends. Making a friend with a person just because they have a car or because their family has money does not make for a genuine friend.
- Don't borrow or lend money if there is no intention of paying the person back. Nothing sours a relationship faster.
- Don't attempt to get a friend to do things that really are not in their best interest, for example, skip homework to hang out, buy something that is really not needed, take drugs or alcohol.
- Don't play stupid practical jokes that may be hurtful and not really funny. No one likes to be made a fool of.
- And, of course, friends don't let friends drive drunk.

The dating game

Now let's talk about dating. The potential for disaster on a teenage date lurks like a hungry alligator in a quiet pond. The dynamics of dating are constantly in flux, especially if you involve friends in the process. Know this: It is not cool to let a friend scout out the terrain for you or, God forbid, do the asking for you. It's been known to happen in which a friend is sent as an emissary with a question such as: "If Lance asked you out on a date, would you go?"

These guidelines might help:

When a boy asks a girl on a date

1. Ask her far enough in advance so she has time to prepare. (Don't let her think she's the last person you called.)
2. Let her know the details: where you're going, when you're going, when you're planning to return, who you're going with.
3. Be on time. (Don't let her worry about being stood up.)
4. See her to the door when you return from the date.

When a girl asks a boy on a date

1. Give him plenty of lead time.
2. Arrange the purchase of tickets ahead of time. ("I've got these two tickets to a concert, or game. Want to go?")
3. Confirm the invitation by writing everything in a note.
4. Be prepared to let it look as though the boy is paying so you don't embarrass him in front of his friends.

While on a date, remember:

1. Be appropriately dressed for each other. (The theory is the bigger the effort you make for a date the more fun it will turn out to be.)
2. Have it completely understood who is paying for what. You can agree to each pay half.
3. Let your parents know where you will be and follow the rules of the more stringent (strict) parent.
4. Be agreeable to the plans that have been made; don't try to change everything around.
5. Don't talk negatively about each other, before, during, or after the date. The guy who moans "I'm stuck with a real

dog for a date tomorrow night" and the girl who complains about being out with a nerd are not class acts.

6. Remember to thank the other person. You can even write him or her a note. Thank his or her parents as well if they provided some service such as food or transportation.

The technology game

When you're among friends—or anywhere else—you need to pay attention to how you use technology.

Cell phones, pagers, and e-mail have made it easier to maintain friendships, but they have also created new etiquette issues. Using a cell phone in public areas—especially in restaurants, theaters, libraries, museums, on public transportation, and even in public restrooms— may be resented by others and even prohibited. Find a private spot for that important conversation. Using a cell phone while driving is not necessarily rude, but it is unsafe and some states are making it illegal. Pull over.

Call-waiting can be used in rude ways. For example, you should never take a second call when someone is in the midst of telling you something personal.

And while we're on the subject of talking on the phone, do you realize that people can hear you typing on your computer while you're talking? Don't do that.

Computer use has guidelines as well. Be as polite with your e-mail as you would be in person. Don't read other people's e-mail. Answer e-mail with a simple "thanks" or other acknowledgment to let people know the message was received. And if you sign off from a chat room or an online video game say "goodbye" to let them know you are leaving. It is rude to simply disappear. E-mail should not be used for sympathy notes or to say thank you for a special gift or favor. Manners experts still favor the postal service.

You can get more information on this subject from *Netiquette* by Virginia Shea (Albion Books, 1994). Or find websites dedicated to the subject by searching for "netiquette" on your favorite search engine.

Chapter 5

How To Feed Your Face

Proper eating etiquette

Teens are great at pigging out. The mission, when it comes to food, is to eat it as rapidly and as efficiently as possible, never mind the mess.

The basics

You have heard all these before (at least I hope so), but they need to be stated again or this book would not be complete:

- Don't talk with your mouth full.
- Chew with your mouth closed.
- Don't lean back in your chair.
- Never point at people with your silverware. It might go off.
- No double-dipping; that is, don't redip celery or carrots or chips or anything else into the dip after you've taken a bite.

Beyond the basics

Someday you may find yourself sitting down to a formal dinner, staring at so much cutlery (silverware) that you feel like you've just landed in a cat burglar's paradise. Spoons, knives, and forks are spread all over.

If you break out in a cold sweat, it is understandable. The situation has all the potential for a disaster. And if your forks have corks on the end of them so you don't hurt yourself, you're really in trouble.

To understand the purpose of all this hardware, you need to know the different courses that are, or can be, served at a formal dinner. While most settings are arranged according to which is used first (start on the outside), some settings are arranged according to size. In that case, you need to know the difference between a fish knife and a meat knife and between a fish fork and a meat fork.

The basic courses are: soup, salad, fish, meat, and dessert.

Throughout this chapter there will be some *do*s and *don't*s for certain situations. For example:

What to Do When:
You sit and see an artfully folded napkin before you?

- *You don't* shake it open like a piece of laundry or tuck it into the neck of your shirt.
- *You do* unfold it calmly and lay it across your lap immediately after sitting down.

The Soup course
Soup may be served from a tureen, or large bowl, and ladled into the bowl at your setting. Food will be served from your left. Dishes will be cleared from the right.

To eat, choose the rounded spoon to the far right. If there is a smaller teaspoon out there, ignore it; it should only be there if you're being served tea. If you realize you've made a mistake, ignore it and keep eating. That is better than calling attention to any mistake you might make in silverware selection.

As you eat, dip the soupspoon away from you to fill, never scoop it toward you. (Do I need to say, "Don't slurp"?) And when the bowl is nearly empty and you want that last tasty portion, tip the bowl away from you to fill your spoon. This way you won't splash the soup on your clothing. Do *not* pick the bowl up and drink out of it.

If it is a formal luncheon, soup may be served in a cup. In this case you may use a smaller soup spoon, if provided, or it may be drunk by lifting the cup.

What to Do When:

You realize you've just put an alien glob of food in your mouth that has the texture of toe jam and a disgusting taste?

- *You don't* spit it out; put it in your napkin, or slip it to the dog.
- *You do* remove it the same way you put it in and deposit it on the edge of your plate (or hide it under the green beans.) If you put it in with a spoon, remove it with a spoon. If you put it in with a fork, remove it with the fork. And if you put it in with your fingers, like an olive with a pit, you may remove it with your fingers.

The Salad course

The salad may be eaten with the salad fork and, yes, a salad knife. If you think the salad can be cut with the side of the fork, it is okay to leave the knife on the table.

Good news: You can use your fingers for some things like asparagus stalks (when the asparagus is served cold in a salad) and artichoke leaves.

If you are at a formal luncheon and the salad is served at the same time as the meat course, it is fine to use the meat fork for the salad.

What to Do When:

You accidentally drop a piece of food on the floor?

- *You don't* call the dog or make a joking comment like, "Hey, it bounced."
- *You do* pick it up and place it on the edge of your plate if it's solid, or ask for a towel to wipe it up if it's something that splats.

The Fish course

The fish course does not need to be complicated. The next knife and fork in from the outside are the tools to use.

The fish will be served from the left and you should take the serving fork in your left hand and the serving spoon in your right hand. Be considerate in taking a small portion and when finished, lay the serving fork and spoon side by side on the platter, never crossed.

If you don't want something, it is okay to politely say "No thank you."

If the fish is boneless, the knife may not be necessary and may be left on the table.

This is a good time to talk about the use of knife and fork. The fish knife is used more delicately than the meat knife. The prongs of the fork should always point down when held in the left hand. When holding the fork in the right hand, the prongs may be up or down. When the fork is in the left hand the knife is used to cut and push. When you are eating with the fork in the left hand, do not put the knife on the plate, leave it on the table. When you are using *only* the fork, hold it in the right hand.

What to Do When:

You've got a piece of fish or other food stuck in your teeth and it's driving you nuts?

- *You don't* make loud sucking noises in an attempt to vacuum it out, pick at it with a fork prong, the pointed blade of a pocket knife, or a hairpin.
- *You do* tough it out without doing a thing because you can't pick your teeth at the table. However, you may ask to be excused.

The Meat course

Now we're getting serious. For this course it's not so much what meat you eat, it's how you eat it. It could be ham, steak, prime rib, pork chops, or a roast. All mouth-watering good—unless you're a vegetarian, in which case you don't have to worry about the meat silverware.

This is the plan of attack. The meat knife is held differently than the fish knife because you need extra leverage to cut. The forefinger can point down the handle.

The fork is for spearing, the knife is for cutting. Remember this: Cut one bite at a time. As efficient as it may be, you shouldn't cut several pieces at once. The good news is you don't need to keep switching the fork to your right hand. Unless you can't help hitting yourself in the forehead or in the chin, it is proper to eat with the left hand. This way you do not have to keep putting the knife down.

This is a good time to talk about silverware signals. Say you want to take a sip of your drink. The silverware should be put down first. The same thing if you wish to use your napkin to dab at your mouth. Do not lay down the knife and fork so that the tips are on the edge of the plate and the handles on the table—as if they were oars on a boat. As long as you are still eating they should be crossed *on* your plate. If your plate is clear and you're hoping for seconds, place the silverware side by side on the *edge* of your plate. If you are finished, place the silverware in the middle of your plate side by side.

What to Do When:
You want to eat the sauce or gravy on your plate?

- *You don't* pick up the plate with both hands and lick it clean.
- *You do* cut bread into a bite-size piece, spear it with your fork, and mop up the gravy, eating the gravy-soaked bread with your fork.

The Dessert course
After the meat course the table will be cleared of all the used stuff. Used silverware, used plates, even the salt and pepper shakers.

A typical dessert serving may begin like this: a plate is served with a fork, spoon, and a bowl of water sitting on a paper doily.

The bowl of water is not thin soup, it's a "finger bowl," used for washing your finger tips when you are finished eating. Remove the finger bowl and place it to the upper left of your plate. Do *not* eat the doily! And do *not* wad it up and throw it at the person across the table. You may place it under the finger bowl.

Dessert may be ice cream, pie, cake, or some other fancy sweet concoction. If it is pie or cake, use your fork. If it's ice cream or, say, a soft burnt cream custard, use your spoon.

When you are finished you may dip the tips of your fingers into the finger bowl. Remember, it's a finger bowl, not a hand bowl, so don't wash your hands. You may brush your lips with wet finger tips and pat dry with your napkin.

What to Do When:
You absolutely have to go potty during dinner?

- *You don't* say something like, "I have to hit the can" or even "I have to go to the bathroom."
- *You do* simply ask, "May I be excused?"

More hints
General guidelines for surviving a formal meal:

- Allow adults to sit before sitting down yourself.
- Pass food to the right. If somebody goofs, don't make them change direction.
- When passing food, hold the plate or bowl so the person next to you can more easily serve himself or herself.
- When food is passed, take small portions making sure there is enough for everyone.
- Don't begin eating until everyone has been served.
- If ordering at a restaurant, don't order the most expensive thing on the menu unless you're buying. Listen to what others are having.
- Wait until the host or hostess signals that your dining experience is over before leaving the table, allowing adults to leave first.

Should You Be Allowed In Public?

Courtesies for the mall, theater, supermarket, and school

It's no secret to adults that most teenagers would rather not be seen in public with their parents. What you may not know is that the reverse is also true. Parents are reluctant to be seen with their teens in public because of the potential for deep embarrassment that lies within the body of every one of you.

Some of that is our fault as adults. Sometimes teenagers decide to be obnoxious, but most of the time they just don't know any better. As one young man from my class put it, "Parents are always telling us to mind our manners, but they never tell us what they are."

Well, here they are. These are common courtesies appropriate in public places:

On the street as pedestrian or driver of a vehicle:

- Don't jaywalk or cross the street against the traffic light.
- Park your car with consideration for others.
- Except in an emergency, forget you have a horn.
- Dim bright lights when other cars approach.
- When driving more slowly than others, stay in the right-hand lane.
- Use the turn signals.
- Don't use your middle finger for anything while driving.

On public transportation:

- Say "hello" to the driver when boarding, and "thank you" when you leave.
- Notify the driver if you see someone running to catch the bus.

- Get up and give your seat to someone (male or female) who is older, disabled, blind, frail, or carrying a child.
- Speak softly, laugh discreetly, and avoid raucous mayhem.

At the movies or the theater:

- Keep quiet once the movie (including the previews) or the performance starts.
- Arrive on time so you don't disturb others in their seats.
- Stay until the end of the performance.
- When moving down a row of people, face the people and not the stage or screen.
- Pick up your candy wrappers, drink and popcorn cartons, and any other trash.

In the supermarket:

- Pick up things that have been knocked off the shelves.
- Maneuver your shopping cart with grace and concern for others.
- When in line with a full cart, let people with one or two items go ahead of you.
- Return shopping carts to the store unless they have return racks in the parking lot.

If you think you have committed some type of no-no, you can always say "excuse me." Say "excuse me" rather than "my bad" or some other expression that adults will not understand. In fact, even if something happens that you know is not your fault, as when somebody accidentally bumps into you, say "excuse me." Do *not* say something along the lines of, "Watch out, dork." That will only generate an angry response in kind and the next thing you know fists (or bullets) may be flying.

Politeness in public matters.

Body Betrayals

Dealing with disaster

Is it possible for a teenager to be embarrassed? Well, sure. Some things that ought to embarrass you don't—because you do them for laughs and maybe to embarrass others. I can't count the number of times I've seen a young man purposely fart in mixed teenage company. Apparently this counts as high humor in teenage circles.

But sometimes your body can betray you. Bobby, John, and Sue climbed into the same bucket on the octopus ride when the carnival came to town. (Note: Bobby had a chili dog just before getting on the ride.) Bobby and Sue were "going together" and John was a friend along for the ride. John was on the left side, Bobby on the right, and Sue in the middle. Bobby put his arm around Sue. It wasn't long before those of us on the ground witnessed a brownish-yellow stream of vomit hurl out and down to the ground below. John, being helpful, yelled out, "Bobby threw up!"

To compound the embarrassment, Bobby did not turn away to barf. He threw up over his arm, which was around Sue at the time, getting vomit on his arm, on the collar of her coat, and all over her long and beautiful light brown hair.

Amazingly, Bobby and Sue continued to date for several years. They got over their embarrassment. The purpose of this chapter is to help you do the same. Things happen. What you need sometimes is damage control. Even President Bush threw up on a Japanese dignitary at a formal dinner. He survived.

What to Do When:
You throw up in public.

- *You don't* leave it.

- *You do* say "excuse me" and make an effort to clean it up. Sensitive, caring friends will help you.

What to Do When:
Someone else throws up in public.

- *You don't* follow suit and throw up yourself, as tempting as that may be.
- *You do* ask if the person is going to be okay and offer to clean up (because you are a sensitive, caring friend).

What to Do When:
You absolutely have to cough because if you try to stop you'll blow steam out your ears.

- *You don't* hack as loud as possible in the direction of the nearest person.
- *You do* cover your mouth.

There are many other body betrayals besides throwing up. Belching, farting, hiccoughing, coughing and, heaven forbid, messing one's pants can all be embarrassing. (Well-mannered people don't do these things on purpose.)

If you've never been in a belching contest, you're just not having any fun. But most of the time, belching in this culture is poor manners. Occasionally, an accidental burp happens. The proper response is to cover your mouth, even if it's too late, and say, "excuse me."

To complicate things, there are burps that smell bad to others. In that case, when you feel one of those burps coming on, roll down your window first or make sure you direct it as far away from people as possible. Funneling it through your nose may help filter the noise and smell, but it could also make your eyes water.

Breaking wind is a polite way of referring to farting. (The formal word is "flatulence.") Please don't make a contest of this bodily function in public. It's okay to laugh among friends when someone passes gas, but don't acknowledge that someone did it in public even if it makes your eyes water or sounded like a gunshot. Even on an elevator. You may feel like you've entered the bog of eternal stench, but don't let on. Be brave. Smile and hold your breath.

People understand hiccoughing. It happens to all of us and is way down the list of embarrassing events. Just don't enhance the hiccough by doing it as loudly as possible. Drinking water helps stop the hiccoughs, especially if someone stands behind you and presses the palms of their hands over your ears while you swallow. Try it next time. It works.

The worst bodily betrayal would be having an accident involving, ahem, number one or number two. Prevention is the better part of the solution. If you are suffering from diarrhea, it is best to avoid going out in public. Skip the rock concert until you get better. The potential negative memory from an accident will outweigh the positive memory of the concert.

If you do have this type of an accident, excuse yourself, leave the scene, and go clean up. This usually means not passing *go*, not collecting $200, but going directly to your home.

Accidents happen so be sympathetic when they happen to other people. When they happen to you, be humble, be apologetic, beware. Always be discreet.

Chapter 8

Growing Up

*What adults can do and you can't
(and why being an adult is, in part,
determined by your behavior)*

When you are told to "grow up and act your age," you might ask: "Well, which is it? Do you want me to grow up or act my age?" When adults ask you to grow up and act your age, what they really want is for you to act more like an adult. It is your behavior, more than your age, that defines you as a grownup.

Having said that, it is important to understand something called "deference," what it means to defer to someone who is older and wiser, and why it is important at this time in your life. There are all sorts of ways of deferring and demonstrating respect to adults. For example, when an adult enters the room, it is polite for you to stand. When adults are talking, you should not interrupt. If you're at the dinner table, pass the food to adults and guests first.

These gestures are all ways of showing respect. Our culture does not demonstrate respect to elders as much as other cultures, and that is too bad. Showing respect to your elders will make the world more pleasant, and—let's not forget the self-interest factor—it will earn you a lot of points. Show adults your respect. Don't sass, act fresh, or defy authority. If someone speaks to you, answer. Politely, of course. Don't maintain sullen silence.

You can also demonstrate respect to your parents and the parents of your friends by helping out around the house, not tracking in mud, picking up after yourself, and so on. When asked to do household chores, do them right away without being asked twice. Be cheerful about it without pouting.

Do you want privacy? So does everyone else. Respect that.

Be on time for appointments. It is rude to make people wait on you.

When you are a passenger in a car, be respectful of the driver.

Adults can legally drink and smoke, and you can't. Because of this, some teenagers believe that drinking and smoking makes them more "grown up." This is an illusion. Most of the time you just look silly. Teenagers who drink usually do so irresponsibly and wind up looking rather pathetic. Drinking alcohol can lead to tragedy, especially when teens are doing the drinking.

You need to understand that the things that are attractive about being an adult—having freedom, having a car, having your own place to live, being able to come and go as you please—come with major responsibilities. To get them you need to hold down a steady job, to pay taxes, to pay bills, to show up on time for appointments, to fix the plumbing when it breaks. If you think you can have the freedom without the responsibility, you're being unrealistic. You have to earn the privileges of adulthood.

Adults who are responsible and who have earned their freedoms should have earned your respect as well. That's why you defer to them and honor them for what they have done. When you become responsible and pay your own way in life—when you're paying for your car, your own insurance, your own house, your own medical bills, your own meals, and so on—then you, too, will generate the respect you've been giving.

So go ahead, act your age. But the more mannerly you are to others, the more you will be perceived as a mature person. The more you are perceived as a mature person, the closer you will be to that adulthood you so crave. I've told you how to get there.

May you live long and prosper.

Bibliography

Baldridge, Letitia. *Letitia Baldridge's Complete Guide to The New Manners for the 90s*. New York: Rawson Associates, 1990.

Hartley, Fred, and Family. *The Teenage Book of Manners ... PLEASE!* Urichsville, Ohio: Barbour Publishing, Inc., 1984.

Hoving, Walter. *Tiffany's Table Manners for Teenagers*. New York: Random House, 1987.

Packer, Alex J. *How Rude! The Teenager's Guide to Good Manners, Proper Behavior, and Not Grossing People Out*. Minneapolis, Minn.: Free Spirit Publishing Inc., 1997.

DEALING WITH LIFE'S DILEMMAS
Exploring Values through English and Drama
Sally-Anne Milgrim

Paper, 224 pp, 5½" x 8½", 0-89390-537-2

Dealing with Life's Dilemmas is a great tool for helping young people explore the emotional and ethical conflicts they face every day. It's a collection of nine plays; each can be performed in a single class period. Themes include seeking independence, family relationships, job hunting, romance, drugs, prejudice, and violence. To aid the student's exploration, each play concludes with an extended series of discussion questions and suggested ways to "play with" the play, including rewriting the ending. One play includes music, another mime; all come with stage directions.

THRILLS AND SKILLS
An Innovative Life-Skills Course for Grades 6–9
Steff Steinhorst

Paper, 128 pp, 8½" × 11", 0-89390-499-6

Study skills. Thinking skills. Manners. Goal-setting. Time-management skills. How do you get adolescents excited about learning these skills? Try *Thrills and Skills*. The "thrills" portion of this course—aided by your own community experts—introduces them to socially acceptable but exciting leisure activities and cranks up their adrenaline flow. The "skills" portion introduces them to the discipline they need to succeed at those and other more mundane activities. This teacher resource includes teaching tips and tricks, session plans, and plenty of handout masters. This is one course your students won't want to miss!

CLASSROOM WARM-UPS
Activities That Improve the Climate
For Learning and Discussion
Dr. Linda Lee Shoop and Deborah Wright

Paper, 86 pp, 8 ½" × 11", 0-89390-477-5

Teens rarely enter a room ready to focus on the subject at hand, especially when they are a captive audience. You first have to get their attention and then you have to change their mood. That's not always easy. *Classroom Warm-Ups* can help. It's filled with teacher-tested, easy-to-use icebreakers and trust-building activities. They are short—they work fast—so they won't interfere with your basic lesson. Use them and watch the atmosphere change. Includes handouts that may be copied.

THE PEER HELPER'S POCKETBOOK
Joan Sturkie and Valerie Gibson

Paper, 104 pp, 4¼" × 7", 0-89390-237-3

Everything needed for effective peer support is here: review of basic communication skills, counseling tips, synopsis of information on issues, and a section for important referral telephone numbers—for those times when more help is indicated.

The Peer Helper's Pocketbook is a quick and easy guide written for peer helpers and counselors on the junior and senior high school and college levels. This small book has proven helpful in both empowering and instructing students. It has come to symbolize responsible peer helping among students everywhere. Put a copy in the faculty room because it is a handy reference for faculty, counselors, and parents.

THE SEVEN HABITS OF PEACEFUL PARENTS
A Facilitator's Manual
Joseph N. Cress, PhD, Elizabeth A. Lonning, PsyD,
Burt Berlowe

Paper, 96 pp, 8½" x 11", 0-89390-512-7

THE PEACEFUL PARENTING HANDBOOK
Burt Berlowe, Elizabeth A. Lonning, PsyD,
Joseph N. Cress, PhD

Paper, 160 pp, 5½" x 8½", 0-89390-513-5

In a world fraught with violence, parents need all the support they can get. These two books can help adult and teenage parents become more confident and better prepared to create a peaceful home. Unlike many programs, this one does not assume there is "one right way" to parent. Instead, it helps parents find the style and techniques that will work best for them—and for their individual children. Use *The Seven Habits of Peaceful Parents* to run a seven-week training course. The parent, meanwhile, can use *The Peaceful Parenting Handbook* as a ready reference of dozens of ways to handle various child-rearing problems.

Order these books from your local bookseller or call:

1-888-273-7782 (toll free) or **1-408-286-8505**

or visit the **Resource Publications, Inc.** website at **www.rpinet.com**.